HOP IT!

Also by Hargreaves

How's That?
Not Out!

strictly for the bird
the bird set
birds of a feather

Hayseeds

For PJ, DJ and Penny

GOOGLIES

by HARGREAVES

Macmillan

SBN Boards: 333 12067 1

First published 1971 by
MACMILLAN LONDON LTD
London and Basingstoke
Associated companies in New York Toronto
Dublin Melbourne Johhannesburg and Madras

Printed in Great Britain by
LOWE AND BRYDONE (PRINTERS) LTD
London

HE SHOULD NEVER HAVE TRIED TO TURN THAT ONE.

" . . . . . *That's it, centre from off the top* . . . .
. . . . . *Right arm over the wicket* . . . .
. . . . . *Six to come* . . . .
. . . . . **YOU ARE ON YOUR OWN!**

HARGREAVES.

HOWZAT-T-T-T-T-T-T-T-T·T··········

HERE ARE TODAY'S CRICKET SCORES
— WILL THOSE WITH
HIGH BLOOD PRESSURE PLEASE
SWITCH OFF.

HE'S UNORTHODOX — BUT WITH AN AVERAGE
OF 153·77 WHO'S TO CRITICISE?

"IN!"

"It's safer here for his first few overs"

HARGREAVES

"HE CAN'T BOWL FOR TOFFEE...."
I REMEMBER YOU SAYING THAT, AS HE GROVELLED
ON THE FLOOR, AMONG THE EMPTIES, PLEADING FOR
A GAME WITH US, AT FRIDAY'S COMMITTEE
MEETING.

HE TURNS UP TODAY TO WATCH —
    VISITORS ARE ONE SHORT —
        — HE BOWLS FOR THEM ......

IF HE WAS A REAL SPORT HE'D
CHUCK HIS WICKET AWAY AND
LET SOME OF US HAVE A BAT
BEFORE WE DECLARE.

HARGREAVES

BOWLED 8 FOR 25 .... SCORED 69 NOT OUT....
WNED 12 BEERS... OUTSANG THE REST UNTIL TWO
THE MORNING... CONVERTED THREE TRIES WITH
E POLICEMAN'S HELMET.
ELCOME, WONDERBOY, TO THE WORLD ON SUNDAY.

COME AND PLAY CRICKET.

NO!

WHY NOT?

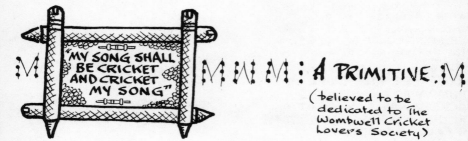

"MY SONG SHALL BE CRICKET AND CRICKET MY SONG"

Ӎ ꟽ Ӎ : A PRIMITIVE. Ӎ

(believed to be dedicated to The Wombwell Cricket Lovers Society)

MAGNIFICENT STYLE!
OH, WHAT A STROKE!
HARD CHEDDAR OLD CHAP!
HEH! HEH!

HARGREAVES

I'D HAVE HAD FOUR SLIPS AT SQUARE LEG AND HE'D HAVE BEEN CAUGHT EARLY ON OFF ONE OF THOSE REBOUNDS OFF THE UMPIRE.

HERCULES FAILS
IN FOURTH TEST!
ATHENS ON TO
A THRASHING
TO NOTHING!
ZEUS
THUNDERBOLTS
WRECK
FOLLOW-ON!
ULYSSES STILL
ON TOUR....

HARGREAVES

al quip in my
1 about the
:h keeps my

Some of the birds who dish up
the teas are dollies

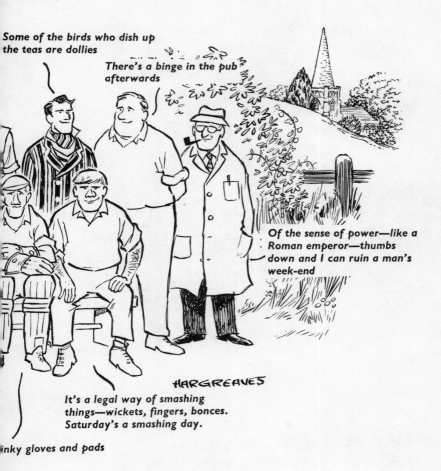

There's a binge in the pub
afterwards

Of the sense of power—like a
Roman emperor—thumbs
down and I can ruin a man's
week-end

HARGREAVES

It's a legal way of smashing
things—wickets, fingers, bonces.
Saturday's a smashing day.

inky gloves and pads

MARRY ME AND DO THE TEAS
FOR THE CLUB ON SATURDAYS.

MISS CRICKET THIS YEAR

CLUB DANCE

Fast Bowler

The Left-Elbow-Well-Up Batting stylist

Outfield

Short Leg

Padded-up Extra Cover

Mid-on

Third Man

HARGREAVES

'IT WASN'T THAT I DIDN'T BELIEVE
— IT'S JUST THAT I WASN'T
SURE .... UNTIL NOW ....'

IF THEE DON'T LIKE
GUARD I'VE TAKEN,
UMPIRE – THEE CAN
COME UP AN' TELL
ME LIKE A MAN –
OR AFTER THE MATCH
WILL DO FINE.

HARGREAVES.

TRADITIONAL SPIRIT

LOCAL PRIDE

IT'S COMPARATIVELY SIMPLE
— YOU REMOVE THE
QUEEN BEE AND THE
OTHERS FOLLOW......

THE COMMITTEE, GEORGE, FEEL WE OUGHT TO
MODERNISE, Y'KNOW.   UPDATE, GET WITH IT.
MECHANICAL AGE, EQUALITY OF THE SEXES AND
ALL THAT.
WE'LL ALL MISS YOU. YOUR SARCASM, YOUR
VULGARITY, YOUR UNFLAGGING IDLENESS
.... GET LOST!

TAKE ANOTHER — NO ONE BACKING UP — LAST WEEK THEY
GOT SLAMMED IN 'THE GAZETTE' FOR LAZINESS IN THE FIELD.

I DON'T THINK WE'VE PLAYED YOU BEFORE,
HAVE WE? THIS IS THE FIRST YEAR WE'VE
PLAYED BEYOND EVERCREECH OR BATCOMBE.

SILENCE REIGNED OVER THE GROUND
.... THE TENSION GREW....
ONLY THE SCRATCHING OF THE SCORER'S
PENS WAS HEARD, REVERBERATING
ACROSS THE PITCH FROM SIGHTSCREEN
TO SIGHTSCREEN, DEAFENING THE
PLAYERS.....

INDIAN CRICKET

Magnificent one, I risk your displeasure, and death by a thousand late-cuts, but the rules do not permit you to have a servant do the run-up if you yourself are bowling.

HARGREAVES

" Peace be with you, Bowler . . . . . .
Strength be in your arm . . . .
Courage be in your heart . . . .
Wisdom be in your head . . . .
But one more bumper from you – – –
And my gun will sing in your ears."

IF YOUR CELESTIAL HIGHNESS
WOULD SHIELD THE GLARE, WHICH
DAZZLES MY UNWORTHY EYES,
FROM THE DIAMOND STUDDED HANDLE
OF HIS JACK HOBBS FIVE STAR
RUBBER SPRUNG "CENTURY·MAKER",
I MIGHT BE ABLE TO SEE CLEARLY
ENOUGH TO GIVE YOUR ALL
GRACIOUS MAJESTY A TRUE
MIDDLE AND LEG FROM
OVER THE TOP!"

'I RECKON SUMMER'S ARE GETTING
COLDER ...... NEXT MAN IN! ...
BIDDLESCOMBE'S COMING OFF WITH
FROSTBITE — AND CLOSE THE DOOR
AS YOU GO.'

UMPIRE'S SIGNALS
(UNOFFICIAL)

I'LL GIVE 5 TO 1 THAT THIS BATSM[...] WILL NOT LAST F[...] ONE OVER.

I ALSO WAS A WOLF CUB BUT I CAN NO LONGER ASSIST YOU TO REMAIN AT YOUR CREASE NOW THAT YOUR REMAINING WICKET IS IN FRAGMENTS.

I AM HOPING T[...] HITCH A LIFT AFT[...] THE GAME IS OVER

DURING THE TEA INTERVAL IN THE PAVILION WE ARE TO BE ENTERTAINED BY A FAN DANCER.

GOOD LORDS! IT BOUNCED FIVE TIME[...] AND HE MISSED IT.

MPIRE'S NOTES ON JUDGING BAD LIGHT.

EMEMBERING THAT CRICKETERS ARE ENTERTAINERS
ND THAT THE SHOW MUST ALWAYS GO ON)

MISTY DARK
IF THE WICKETS CAN BE SEEN AND SHAPES OF THE PLAYERS DISCERNED THEN THE GAME MUST CONTINUE.

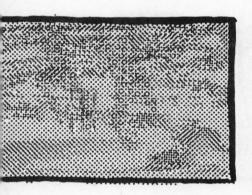

MURKY DARK
IF IT IS POSSIBLE TO HEAR YELLS OF ANGUISH FROM THE BATTING END EACH TIME THE BOWLER RUSHES BY THEN THE GAME SHOULD CONTINUE.

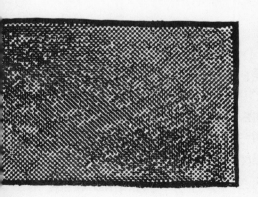

MUCKY BLACK
AT THIS POINT THE UMPIRES SHOULD CONFER (IF THEY CAN FIND EACH OTHER). IT IS UNLIKELY THEY WILL DECIDE TO CONTINUE IN THESE CONDITIONS FOR IT IS PROBABLE THEY ARE THE ONLY ONES LEFT ON THE FIELD.

'..THE BAT CAME DOWN ON THE BALL WITH
A CRACK WHICH PIERCED THE STAR STUDDED VAULT
OF THE SKY AND THE STAR STUDDED FIELD OF THE
AUSTRALIANS ... THE EARTH CRACKED AND SPLIT...
HOBBS HAD BLOWN THE LAST TRUMPET OF THE
DAY OF JUDGEMENT... THE LION'S ROAR CAME
FROM THE BLOWING BUGLE. WE HAD WON
THE ASHES FROM THE AUSSIES.'

AT THE NETS   HARGREAVES

HARGREAVES.

THAT'S IT —
HIS SLOW ONE —
IT FOOLS THEM ALL.

HARGREAVES

I'M ON STRIKE, SKIPPER — TILL YOU LET
ME HAVE A BOWL — DOWN THE SLOPE —
WIND BEHIND ME — IN FAILING LIGHT —
AGAINST THE TAIL ENDERS — EVERY
MATCH — ALL THIS SEASON.

SUPER PERFUME ISN'T IT?
IT'S CALLED 'GLANCE TO LEG'.

The Classical Cut

THAT'S DEFINITELY THE
LAST TIME I PLAY A
STRAIGHT BAT....
....EVER.

AN INSIDE JOB, EH? WE SHOULD STAND
A GOOD CHANCE ON SATURDAY
WITH THEIR BEST BAT GONE .....
..... WELL DONE LILLYWHITE.

Annual Christmas Duck Hunt

Acknowledgements

The artist and publisher are grateful to V. Patta-
bhiraman Esq of Madras for permission to repro-
duce the drawings on pages 1, 44–48; to *The
Cricketer* for those on pages 40–41, 60 (bottom) and
63; and to *Punch Publications Ltd* for those on pages
8–9, 24–25, 56–57.